Songs of Love, Music, and Nature

10 Contemporary Solos for Female Voice and Piano

Compiled and Edited by Sally K. Albrecht

Contents	Page
1. Autumn	3
Words and Music by Andy Beck	
2. The Moon	7
Words and Music by Andy Beck	
3. Mother, Please Explain	12
Traditional French Country Song, from a setting by J. B. Weckerlin	
English translation by Sigmund Spaeth, Arranged by John Lewers	
4. Music Speaks	18
Words and Music by Michael Adler and Brad Green, Arranged by Andy Beck	
5. Oh, No!	22
Words by Thomas Haynes Bayley, Music by Ruth Morris Gray	
6. Poor Boy	28
American Folk Song, Arranged by Ruth Elaine Schram	
7. Remember My Song	33
Words and Music by Sally K. Albrecht and Jay Althouse	
Violin part	39
8. Shooting Star	40
Words and Music by Andy Beck	
9. Why Does the Willow Tree Weep?	44
Words and Music by Andy Beck	
Oboe/C-instrument part	50
10. WinterSong	51
Words by John Parker, Music by Vicki Tucker Courtney	

© 2010 Alfred Music Publishing Co., Inc.
All Rights Reserved. Printed in USA.

Photographs: Tim Hayden–Nashville, TN

Book (32935)	ISBN-10: 0-7390-6475-4	ISBN-13: 978-0-7390-6475-7
Accompaniment CD (32936)	ISBN-10: 0-7390-6477-0	ISBN-13: 978-0-7390-6477-1
Book & CD (32937)	ISBN-10: 0-7390-6476-2	ISBN-13: 978-0-7390-6476-4

**All of the solos in this collection are also available as Alfred choral arrangements.
Visit alfred.com for more information.**

Autumn
Andy Beck
SATB 23038
3-Part Mixed 23039
SSA 23040
2-Part 28719
SoundTrax CD 28733
SoundPax 28734

The Moon
Andy Beck
2-Part 28541

Mother, Please Explain
Arranged by John Lewers
SSA (Bergerettes #2) 28736

Music Speaks
Michael Adler, Brad Green/Andy Beck
SATB 27256
SAB 27257
2-Part 27258
SoundTrax CD 27259

Oh, No!
Thomas Haynes Bayley, Ruth Morris Gray
SSA 31175

Poor Boy
Arranged by Ruth Elaine Schram
SSA 31079

Remember My Song
Sally K. Albrecht, Jay Althouse
SATB 31152
SAB 31153
SSA 31154
TBB 31155

Shooting Star
Andy Beck
2-Part 30961

Why Does the Willow Tree Weep?
Andy Beck
SATB 23969
3-Part Mixed 23970
SSA 23971

WinterSong
John Parker, Vicki Tucker Courtney
SATB 27260
3-Part Mixed 27261
SSA 27262

1. AUTUMN

Words and Music by
ANDY BECK

gone. Au-tumn leaves are float-ing from the trees,

or - ange, yel - low, red, and brown._____ Au - tumn leaves are danc - ing

with the breeze, au - tumn leaves are drift - ing down.

Sum - mer

37 Au - tumn leaves are danc - ing with the breeze, au - tumn leaves are drift - ing

40 down. 41 *f* Au - tumn leaves are float - ing.

43 *rit. e decresc.* Au - tumn leaves are danc - ing. Au - tumn leaves are drift - ing,

46 **Slowly** *p* *in tempo* *pp* danc - ing, float - ing, float - ing down.

2. THE MOON

Words and Music by
ANDY BECK

lis - ten - ing? O moon, sil - ver - y and bright,

come a-gain to-mor - row night, come a-gain to-mor - row night.

Day - light is com - ing soon.

Where will you go, O moon? Un - der a cloud? O - ver a hill?

See you to-mor-row night, I will.

moon, O moon. O moon, O moon. O

moon. Moon.

3. MOTHER, PLEASE EXPLAIN

Traditional French Country Song
English translation by **SIGMUND SPAETH**

From a setting by **J. B. WECKERLIN**
Arranged by **JOHN LEWERS**

come to me and swear That he loved me well.
ju - ré l'au - tre jour Qu'il m'ai - mait_____ bien.

How could I tell? How could I tell? If he should
Je ne dis rien. Je ne dis rien. Mais s'il re -

come and say the same a - gain, What shall I an - swer then?_____ What
vient en - cor m'en dire au - tant, Que faire a - lors, ma - man?_____ Que

shall I an - swer then?
faire a - lors, ma - man?

4. MUSIC SPEAKS

Arranged by
ANDY BECK

Words and Music by
MICHAEL ADLER *and* **BRAD GREEN**

weak. When we can't find_____ the words we seek, when all words

fail,_____ still mu - sic speaks, when all words fail,

still mu - sic speaks. Mu - sic

speaks._____

5. OH, NO!

Words by
THOMAS HAYNES BAYLEY (1797-1839)

Music by
RUTH MORRIS GRAY

sport to sport they hur-ry, hur-ry me, to ban-ish my re-gret; And

2nd time to CODA $\oplus$
(p. 26, m. 57)

when they win a smile from me, they think that I for-get. For-

get, for-get, they think that I for-get. Oh, no!

They

24

6. POOR BOY

American Folk Song

Arranged by
RUTH ELAINE SCHRAM

sweet - heart stood on the deck of one, where she waved to

you good - bye. Bow down your head and

cry, poor boy, bow down your head and cry;

and stop think - ing of the one you love, bow

fought a duel for her hon-or, poor boy, you fought from morn 'til night._____ You won her heart, but a-gain, you would part; good-bye, poor boy, good-bye._____ Bow down your head and cry, poor boy, bow down your

*Dedicated to Daniel Pearl World Music Days***

7. REMEMBER MY SONG

Words and Music by
SALLY K. ALBRECHT
and **JAY ALTHOUSE**

* Violin part, with bowings, is on page 39.

** Daniel Pearl Music Days is a global network of concerts that conveys the message of "Harmony for Humanity."
Please visit *danielpearlmusicdays.org* for more information.

Re-mem-ber my words,
My song is your song.

re-mem-ber my voice.
And when we're a - part,

Re-mem-ber my thoughts,
my voice is your voice;

re-mem-ber my choice.
my heart is your heart.

Re-mem-ber my touch,
Re-mem-ber my life,

re-mem-ber my goal.
and al-ways be strong.

Re-mem-ber my dream, and re-mem-ber my
Re-mem-ber my love, and re-mem-ber my

soul, my soul.
song, my

song. Life takes us on a jour-ney, our

111

111111111111

111111111111111

re-mem-ber._____ Re-mem-ber my words,

re-mem-ber my voice. Re-mem-ber my thoughts,

re-mem-ber my choice. Re-mem-ber my life,

38

Dedicated to Daniel Pearl World Music Days

7. REMEMBER MY SONG

VIOLIN

Words and Music by
SALLY K. ALBRECHT
and **JAY ALTHOUSE**

With feeling (♩ = ca. 108-112)

NOTE: The purchase of this book carries with it the right to photocopy this page.

8. SHOOTING STAR

Words and Music by
ANDY BECK

9. WHY DOES THE WILLOW TREE WEEP?

Words and Music by
ANDY BECK

* Oboe/C instrument part is on page 50.

Why do the branch - es quiv - er as they sweep, why does the wil - low tree

weep? _____

Why does the wil - low tree cry? What sad - ness is lin - ger - ing

* cleave - hold fast, stick to, or cling

9. WHY DOES THE WILLOW TREE WEEP?

OBOE *(optional C-instrument)*

Words and Music by
ANDY BECK

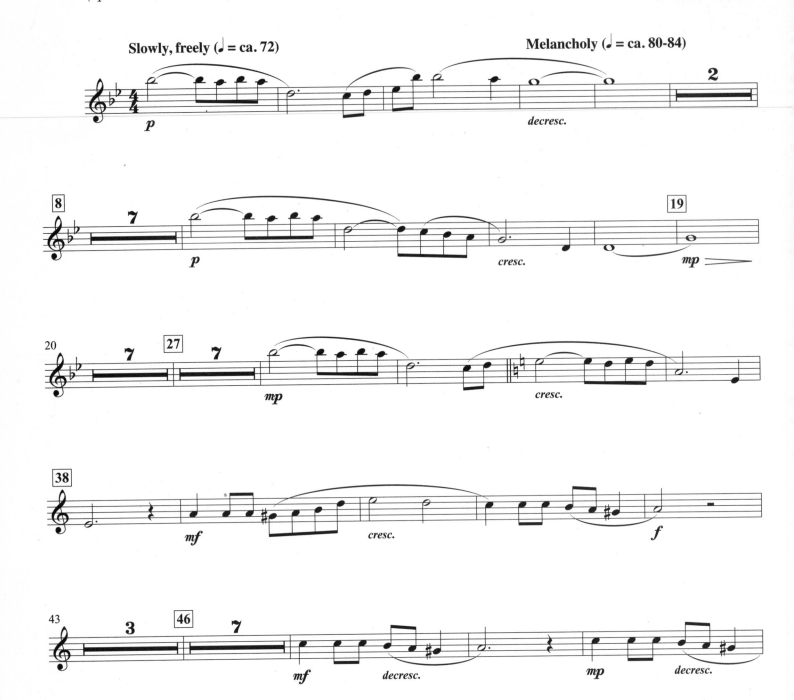

NOTE: The purchase of this book carries with it the right to photocopy this page.

10. WINTERSONG

Lyrics by
JOHN PARKER (ASCAP)

Music by
VICKI TUCKER COURTNEY (ASCAP)

Here be-neath the snow-y cov-er, fall-en at the win-ter's trea-son,

lik-ened not to an-y oth-er, lies the trac-es of a sea-son.

flown. Bit - ter ic - y fro - zen fin - gers laid the blow a - cross his

chin. Au - tumn bur - ied deep - ly un - der is

like - ly not to rise a - gain, a - gain!

Gone the pur - ple, gone the gold - en, blown a - way to worlds un -

Enjoy these additional Alfred vocal collections—just for the ladies!

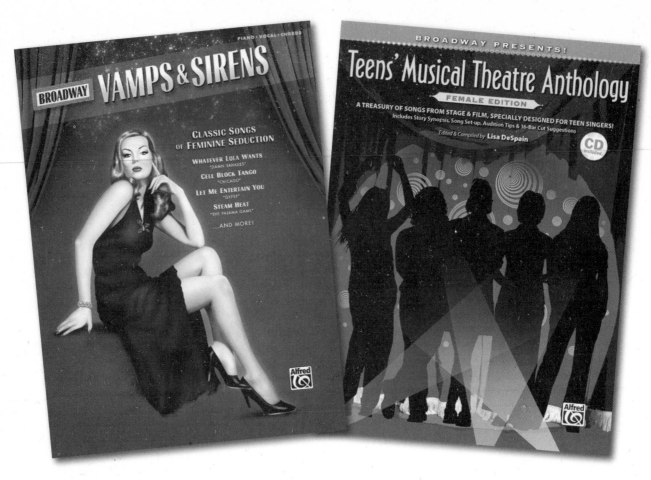

BROADWAY VAMPS & SIRENS
Classic Songs of Feminine Seduction

Enjoy these 37 classic songs sung of feminine seduction and naughtiness from the best of musical theater.

Titles include: And All That Jazz (*Chicago*) • Flaming Agnes (*I Do! I Do!*) • Follow Me (*Camelot*) • Let Me Entertain You (*Gypsy*) • My Heart Belongs to Daddy (*Leave It to Me!*) • Shady Lady Bird (*Best Foot Forward*) • That'll Show Him (*A Funny Thing Happened…*) • Whatever Lola Wants (*Damn Yankees*) • and many more.

   Book   29182

BROADWAY PRESENTS!
TEENS' FEMALE VOCAL ANTHOLOGY
Edited by Lisa DeSpain

Don't miss this delightful collection of over 30 musical theater songs from a variety of shows that span decades of theater history. Using the original vocal scores, the songs have been selected and adapted with the ranges and skills of teen singers in mind. Authoritative historical and contextual commentary, audition tips, and 16-bar cut suggestions for each song make this the most useful and relevant collection of its kind. CD includes accompaniment tracks.

Titles include: Always True To You in My Fashion (*Kiss Me, Kate*) • Boy Wanted (*My One and Only*) • Gimme Gimme (*Thoroughly Modern Millie*) • I Speak Six Languages (*The 25th Annual Putnam County Spelling Bee*) • Mama Who Bore Me (*Spring Awakening*) • The New Girl in Town (*Hairspray*) • Show Me (*My Fair Lady*) • Your Daddy's Son (*Ragtime*) • and many more.

   Book/CD   32024

Visit alfred.com for more information and a complete listing of vocal collections.